Other books in the well-defined series by Henry Beard & Roy McKie

sailing: a sailor's dictionary
fishing: an angler's dictionary
gardening: a gardener's dictionary
cooking: a cook's dictionary
golfing: a duffer's dictionary

A SKIER'S DICTIONARY

skiing

A SKIER'S DICTIONARY

BY HENRY BEARD
& ROY McKIE

WORKMAN PUBLISHING
NEW YORK

Library of Congress Cataloging-in-Publication Data

Beard, Henry.
    Skiing: a skier's dictionary/by Henry Beard and Roy McKie.
       p. cm.
    ISBN 0-89480-650-5 : $5.95
    1. Skis and skiing—Humor.   2. Skis and skiing—Terminology—
Humor.   I. McKie, Roy.   II. Title.
GV854.3.B37   1989
796.93'0207—dc20   89-40369

Workman Publishing Company
708 Broadway
New York, New York 10003

Manufactured in the United States of America

First printing October 1989

10 9 8 7 6 5 4 3 2

To all those who have heard the call of the slopes.

A

Aerials	Competitive form of ski jumping in which daredevil skiers attempt various midair acrobatics such as somersaults, back flips, and body twists. Points are awarded on the basis of the length of the hospital stay, the size of the bill, the originality of the x-rays, the degree of difficulty of the surgery, and the creativity displayed in filling out the insurance claim as measured by the speed and size of payment. *See* HOTDOGGING.
Alp	*1.* One of a number of ski mountains in Europe. *2.* A shouted request for assistance made by a European skier in America. An appropriate reply is "What's Zermatter?"
Alpine	The formal descriptive term for downhill skiing, one of the four basic ski techniques. The other three are nordic (cross-country skiing), norpine (downhill skiing on cross-country equipment), and asinine (snowboarding).
Altitude Sickness	In addition to the common symptoms of headache, dizziness, vertigo, nausea, and insomnia, subtler physical conditions brought on by breathing the oxygen-poor atmosphere at high-altitude ski resorts include a love of being cold (Nansen's Disease), an indifference to heights (the Icarus Complex), a compulsion to apply wax to things (Tussaud's Complaint), an impulse to wear ugly or silly clothing (Bozo's Syndrome), and an urge to immediately dispose of any excess cash (Rocky Mountain Ski Shop Fever).
American Teaching Method	A simplified, accelerated system of ski instruction in which students are taught how to operate a hot tub before they learn the snowplow.

Angulation

The ideal balanced posture for standing on or traversing a slope, in which the hips and knees are thrust inward toward the hill while the head and torso are angled outward and downhill in a curved position known as the "banana" or "comma." A more common posture is one in which the skier's whole body is leaned directly into the hill as far away as possible from any downward direction in a position known as the "Idon'twanna" or "Momma!"

Anticipation

The first of six basic phases of the classic ski turn. It is followed by Initiation, Trepidation, Desperation, Exclamation, and Recuperation. *See* TURN.

Après-ski

Descriptive term for activities in a ski resort in the evening following a day on the slopes. Typical of these are le bitch and la moan, le stiff drink, le soaking des tootsies, le long nap, le big wait at le fancy dump for la lousy meal, beaucoup de wondering why le hell we do this stuff, and le checking on la airline to see if they have le earlier flight home.

Artificial Snow

Man-made snow produced by forcing a jet of water or an air-and-water mixture out of a nozzle under very high pressure. The snowmaking process creates a slope surface indistinguishable from a real snowfall in all but one respect: even the lightest sleepers at a ski resort generally will not sit bolt upright in bed at 5:00 A.M. if a couple of inches of natural snow begin to fall.

Avalanche

One of the very small number of actual perils that skiers face and that needlessly frighten timid individuals away from the sport. *See also* BLIZZARD, CONTUSION, FRACTURE, FROSTBITE, GONDOLA PLUNGE, HYPOTHERMIA, LIFT COLLAPSE, POLE PUNCTURE, SNOWMOBILE MISHAP, WHITEOUT, and YETI.

Après-ski

Big Foot

B

Bare Spot

A place where, due to insufficient snowfall, the underlying earth is visible. Depending on weather conditions, bare spots can range from a patch the size of a footprint to a patch the size of the eastern United States.

Base

1. The layer of plastic on the bottom of a ski that is no longer there because 2. The layer of snow on the surface of a slope is no longer there.

Bastard

1. A wide, flat, single-cut file used to flatten and sharpen ski edges. 2. Someone who charged you for hand-filing your ski edges but used a belt-sander instead.

Belt Bag

A small zippered bag, sometimes also called a fanny pack, which is attached to the waist by a belt and positioned just above the rump. It is a superb shock absorber for bruising backward falls since it is usually filled with a dense, pasty, body-cushioning substance made of suntan lotion that has leaked from the tube, crushed candy bars, a wad of sticky money, and a burst packet of hand-warmer fluid.

Bent Ski Poles

1. Expert skiers' poles shaped at the factory to fit around the body and thus reduce wind resistance. 2. Beginning skiers' poles shaped during use to fit around trees, trail signs, and chairlift pylons.

Big Foot

Giant, hairy-bodied reclusive humanoid said to live in remote mountain areas. Such creatures probably do not exist, but if they do and they ever decide to take up skiing, they're in luck because ski-equipment rental shops have a remarkably large selection of boots that appear to have been designed for their exclusive use.

Bindings

Ingenious automatic mechanisms that attach the skis to the ski boots at the heel and toe. Bindings very effectively protect skiers from potentially serious injury during a bad fall by releasing the ski from the boot, sending it skittering across the slope where it trips another skier, who avoids serious injury when his bindings release, allowing his skis to spring loose and trip two other skiers, who fall, causing their bindings to release before they suffer serious injury, sending their skis into the path of four other skiers, and so on, eventually causing the entire slope to be closed, thus protecting every skier in the area from serious injury.

Bones

There are 206 bones in the human body. While this statement of potential vulnerability may dismay some skiers, particularly novices, it is worth noting that according to medical records two of them, the left and right stapes of the inner ears, have never been broken in any reported skiing accident.

Boogy

To ski flat out; one of several terms that surfing has contributed to skiing. Skiing terms, however, have not found their way to the beach, partly because of the lack of appeal of the basic "schusser" look (a runny nose, chapped lips, and a major limb in a cast) and partly because the Franco-German sources of most skiing expressions have poor substitutes for such pithy, snappy terms as "bummer" (Oh, dîtes-donc, quel grand malheur), "far out" (Träumerisch), "hot dog" (Bockwurst), "cool" (bien refraî-chisse), "go for it" (allez, faîtes la tentative), "cruising" (la grande descente dans le style de la croisière), and "wipe-out" (Ausradierung).

Boot

See PAIN.

Boot Fit   *1.* The extent to which a ski boot is the right size or shape for a foot. *2.* A highly emotional outburst caused by wearing ski boots that are the wrong size or shape.

Bump   *1.* A swelling resulting from *2.* A blow caused by tripping over *3.* An elevated mound of snow. *See* MOGUL.

C

Cable Car   An aerial tramway consisting of heavy, pylon-supported cables strung very far above the ground from which is suspended a large cabin capable of carrying over a hundred skiers on a fast, steep ascent to a high-altitude skiing area. It is most common in Europe, where it is known as the Téléférique, the Horrorférique, or the Petriférique.

Camber   A built-in arch or convexity found in all skis, varying in depth of curve among different models and manufacturers. Other areas of variation in ski design include "side-cut," the degree of taper in the waist; "splay," the steepness of curve of the tip; "flex," the amount of torsional movement in the body of the ski; "damping," the ability of the ski to limit vibration; "swingweight," the weight distribution over the ski's length; "repellence," the ugliness of coloration, trademarks, and designs on the top of the ski; "shameface," the degree of embarrassment caused by the cheapness of the ski; "flingstrength," the ski's resistance to mishandling by airline personnel; "scathe," the rate of deterioration of the ski when dumped in a hall closet; "swipe-risk," the ski's desirability to a thief; and "searchlength," the amount of time its owner would spend looking for it in deep snow at the edge of a trail at 4 o'clock on a Sunday afternoon.

Carrying Skis

Even when held tightly together by straps or interlocking brakes, a pair of skis is awkward to manage. To master the knack of carrying them, have a friend stand close behind you on your right or left side. Place the skis over your shoulder, with the tips forward and the bindings just touching your back, and drape your arm over their top surface. Now pivot on your hips slowly in both directions as if looking at the scenery. The last foot or so of your skis should hit your friend smartly at about ear level. If you're grazing the top of his head or just nudging him somewhere around his belt, adjust your grip, increase the speed of your hip turn, or flatten the slope of the ski-carrying angle.

Carved Turn

A high-speed skidless parallel turn made with minimum body movement; the aspiration of obsessive skiers.

Cast

A high-strength rigid plaster dressing designed for minimum body movement; the destination of obsessive skiers.

Catching an Edge

Accidentally letting the edge of a ski dig into the snow; one of the 640 most common causes of falls in skiing.

Chairlift

A transportation system in which a series of chairs suspended from a cable rapidly conveys 1, 2, 3, or 4 skiers at a time from the front of one lift line to the rear of another.

Check

1. A braking maneuver on a steep hill which requires skiers to flex their knees, push their hips into the snow, make a fast upward hopping movement, and head into the next turn. 2. A backbreaking ski village restaurant bill which causes all the skiers at a table to flex their knees, push their hips against the backs of their chairs, set their feet flat on the floor, make a fast upward hopping movement, and head for the door.

Compound Fracture

Christie

Term for any skidded turn that ends with the skis in a parallel position. The maneuver was introduced and perfected by Norwegians who named it for Norway's capital city, Christiania, from which it was eventually contracted to "christie." In 1925, reacting to a wave of public revulsion at the perversion of pure nordic skiing technique by downhill-crazed foreigners who were experimenting with such horrors as the stem Christiania and the scissor Christiania, Norway's parliament, the Storting, voted to change the name of the capital to something completely unrelated to the new so-called sport of alpine skiing. Oslo was the final choice, but interestingly, on the long list of runners-up were Lippbålm, Velkrø, Däyglǒ, Måmbo, Pømä, and Demó, and Tåhøe, Altå, Äspenn, and Støwe.

Citizen Race

A marathon open to amateur or recreational nordic skiers. The most famous are the 53-mile Vasaloppet in Sweden and the 22-mile Birkebeiner in Wisconsin, but a pair of lesser known, more informal yet equally demanding races are growing in popularity: Vermont's grueling Saabslog, in which teams of cross-country skiers have to tow a disabled vehicle from a ski resort parking lot to a gas station 14 miles away, and Colorado's Baggageblunder, in which skiers on ill-fitting rental equipment ski a special 18-mile circuit around the Denver airport looking for their lost luggage.

Code

1. A set of rules governing how a skier should behave on the slopes. *2.* A stuffed-up node that a skier cad get from staddig aroud id wet clode id a lift lide.

Compound Fracture

One of the two worst things that someone can end up with in a ski area.

Condo

The other.

Convenience Boot	Term for a rear-entry design alpine ski boot which has an internal cable system that makes it possible for a skier to produce total discomfort over the entire foot with a single preset lever.
Conventional Boot	Term for a front-entry design alpine ski boot which has a number of micro-adjustable buckles that make it possible for a skier to produce a welt, bruise, blister, or pinch at any desired point on the foot.
Cross-country Skiing	Traditional Scandinavian all-terrain snow-traveling technique. It isn't difficult to learn, nor is it dangerous. It's good exercise, but it isn't strenuous or likely to cause injuries. Its equipment isn't complex, uncomfortable, or particularly expensive. It doesn't require the purchase of costly lift tickets, and it doesn't involve rides on aerial transport devices. It has no crowds or lines. It doesn't attract rich twerps or adolescent jerks. Snow bunnies make fun of it. Snowboarders shun it. It isn't skiing. *See* CROSS-COUNTRY SOMETHING-OR-OTHERING.
Cross-country Something-or-othering	Recreational cross-country touring on skis, usually along trails in scenic wilderness areas. More and more skiers have discovered the pleasures of gliding through the silent, peaceful, snow-hushed woods, far from the noise and crowds of the ski slopes, moving with the restful rhythm of the classical nordic step, with no sound but the whispery hiss of the skis slipping through the snow, the soft slapping of the loose backpack flap, the muffled tinkle of the car keys dropping into the puffy powder of a deep, wind-sculpted drift, the sharp, crisp snap of a ski binding breaking, and the eerie wail of elemental rage as man comes to grips with the ancient force of nature.

Day Area

D

Daily Ski Report

A printed or broadcast description of the local snow cover at a given ski area based on information provided by its managers. Since slope surfaces can vary considerably, skiers should be familiar with a few common terms used by resorts to describe local conditions: packed powder (wet slush), packed powder (glare ice), packed powder (frozen granules), packed powder (breakable crust), and packed powder (a light dusting of snow on mostly bare earth).

Day Area

A skiing facility without overnight accommodations where, after spending several hours dodging the dolts on the slopes, you get to spend several hours dodging the dolts on the roads.

Destination Resort

A full-service skiing facility that offers not just lift lines, but also locker lines, front desk lines, elevator lines, shuttle-bus lines, restaurant lines, and movie lines.

DIN

Deutsche Industrie-Norm, or German Industrial Standard, a set of internationally accepted standards that includes the settings for ski bindings. A chart produced by German engineers provides for ski shops precise instructions on setting the release point for toe and heel bindings based on the weight, physical structure, and bone strength of individual skiers, their grooming and personal hygiene, their posture while standing at strict attention, their knowledge of the applicable rules and regulations, their overall cooperativeness with the proper authorities, and their readiness at all times to do exactly as they are told without sniveling like the miserable, inferior weaklings they are.

Double Black Diamond
Trail-marking symbol indicating a very difficult run for experts only, with slopes greater than 40% or 22° that is generally skied by skiers with skis no less than 180cm long and IQs no higher than 75. *See* TRAIL RATING.

Double Boot
A modern, two-piece ski boot, designed so that the part that won't close correctly is separate from the part that doesn't fit properly. *See* INNER BOOT and OUTER SHELL.

Double-pole Push
A method of crossing flat terrain by propelling oneself forward using both ski poles at the same time. Making this powerful pushing motion is strenuous, but it does help develop the muscles skiers will need at the end of a ski trip to cram 90 pounds of lumpy, puffy ski equipment into a couple of suitcases and still have plenty of upper-arm strength left over to beat their fists in rage on the counters of the hotel front desk, the rental car office, and the airline.

Down
Polite synonyms for the act and result of falling should always be employed. For "down," use "unup" or "formerly perpendicular"; for "to fall," substitute "pronificate," "supinize," or "recumbify"; and instead of "fall," say "snow check," "slope pause," or "whole-body surface contact."

E

Edging
1. Vital skiing skill that involves using a rolling motion of the knees and hips to tilt the ski edges into the slope, making it possible to stand still on the fall line. *2.* Vital skiing skill that involves using a series of hip movements and shoulder turns to thrust the body slowly forward, making it possible to gain several places in the lift line.

Egg

Egg	Name for a crouched or tucked body position used by skiers to eliminate wind resistance on a fast, straight downhill run. It is often followed by the Dropped Egg, the Egg Roll, and the Omelet.
Elasticity	The ability of a ski binding to permit some toe and heel movement before releasing, usually measured in terms of RCT (return to center time). The other basic measures of a binding's quality are its RSA (how long before it is returned to the store for adjustment), its TBSS (time before something goes *sproing*), DSBF (days in a shop being fixed), and NTSSASS (number of times skier swears at the salesman who sold it to him).
Exercises	It is important to be in proper physical condition before going skiing. Here are a few simple exercises you can do to make sure you're prepared for the slopes: • Stand in one place for five minutes, then take two steps forward. Repeat 10 times. • Attach a cinderblock to each foot with old belts or rope and walk up and down a flight of stairs. • Sit on a second-story window ledge with your skis on and your poles in your lap for 30 minutes. • Tie your legs together at the ankles and lie flat on the floor; then, holding a banana in each hand, get to your feet. • Grasp a credit card in your non-writing hand, then sign your name 100 times.

F

Fall	*1.* A poor season for skiing. *2.* A good reason for not skiing.

Exercises: The Basic Pre-ski Workout

THE FACE PLANT
(10 REPETITIONS)

THE CHAIRLIFT SQUAT
(20 REPETITIONS)

THE BACK FLOP (5 REPETITIONS)

AEROBIC WORKOUT ON THE SCHUSSCYCLE (15 MINUTES)

Fall Line

An imaginary line following the steepest and most direct path down any given slope. Skiers executing turns and traverses constantly pass across the fall line as they make their way downhill, often stopping for a while at other imaginary boundary marks like the Topple Corridor, the Tumble Lane, the Stagger Path, and the Stumble Zone.

Fear

See ICE.

Finnish Step

1. A cross-country skiing technique used by racers to rest their muscles in which the pole plant is left out on every second or third stride. Also known as the "swinging step" or "triple striding." *2.* A cross-country skiing technique used by skiers who have to go to the bathroom badly in which a series of very short, almost hopping steps are made with the knees held close together. Also known as the "squirming step," "Finnish two-step," or "nordic twitch."

Freestyle Mogul Skiing

A skiing event in which competitors are judged on their speed, style, and control as they race down steep, heavily moguled slopes to the sound of prerecorded music of their choice. For some reason, most "bump skiers" choose the music of the Rolling Stones as accompaniment, particularly the tunes "Shattered," "Twisted," "Please, Doctor, I'm Damaged," and "Let It Bleed."

G

Geländesprung

German term for a daring aerial maneuver in which a skier jumps from the edge of a bump, ridge, or slope in order to clear an obstacle by leaping over it. The word is pronounced "godDAMNwhataSTUPIDthingtoDO."

Gravity

Gloves   Skiers' hand coverings that have precisely calibrated thermal layers to provide excessive warmth on hotter days and insufficient heat on colder ones; that are designed to be tight enough around the back of the hand and wrist to restrict circulation but not to be so close-fitting on the fingers as to allow any discernible manual dexterity; that are able to admit moisture from the outside without permitting any dampness within to escape; and that are bulky enough to ensure that they won't fit into any known pocket while still being light enough to be easily knocked or blown off a lap if removed during a ride on a chairlift.

Goggles   Eye-protection device that greatly reduces the sun's potentially damaging glare by using a tiny amount of trapped moisture to produce, directly in front of the wearer's eyes, a dense layer of light-absorbing fog.

Gondola   A ski lift consisting of a series of small, enclosed, somewhat cramped cabins suspended from a continuously moving overhead cable to which they are engaged by an operator once they are fully loaded. It is a fast and easy way to go up the mountain unless you suffer from acrophobia (fear of heights), claustrophobia (fear of confined spaces), fatsophobia (fear of being sat on by a corpulent person), gabbophobia (fear of having to make conversation with a dolt), velcrophobia (fear of becoming permantly attached to someone else's pocket flap), or autoparkasphyxiaphobia (fear of being smothered by one's own down ski jacket).

Gravity   One of the four basic forces that affect skiers. The others are the strong force, which jams their bindings; the weak force, which causes their ankles to wobble; and electromagnetism, which makes their car batteries go dead.

Grip & Glide	The two basic actions of a properly waxed nordic ski.
Gripe & Grouse	The two basic actions of a nordic skier on improperly waxed skis.

H

Hat	Any of several types of soft, insulating headgear worn by skiers. As a rule, skiers do not wear hard-shelled, impact-proof helmets to prevent head injuries. This may be because any individual who believes it's fun descending a steep slope at a high rate of speed on a cold day clearly lacks a vital organ above the neck that requires protection.
Heli-skiing	A form of off-trail skiing in which skiers are transported by helicopter to the summits of remote mountains without ski lifts. Heli-skiing has the advantage of providing pristine, deep-powder slopes and no lift lines, but the absence of facilities does turn some people off, particularly those who are concerned by the problems inherent in heli-going-to-the-bathroom, heli-finding-a-lost-ski, and heli-walking-all-the-way-down while heli-freezing-to-death.
Herringbone	A method for ascending a slope in which a skier plants his skis into the snow with the tails together and the tips apart and climbs with short, duck-walking steps. This maneuver can be tiring and time-consuming, but it has its advantages: you never have to look down the fall line, nobody ever wants to race you, you don't need to do anything fancy to come to a full stop, and you have at least 20 minutes from the time you first see a tree until the moment you hit it.

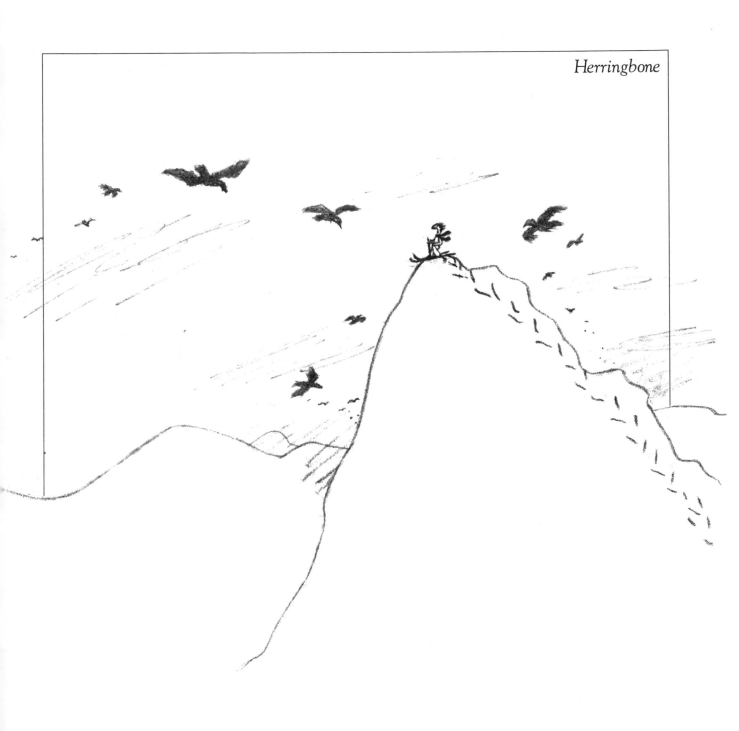

Herringbone

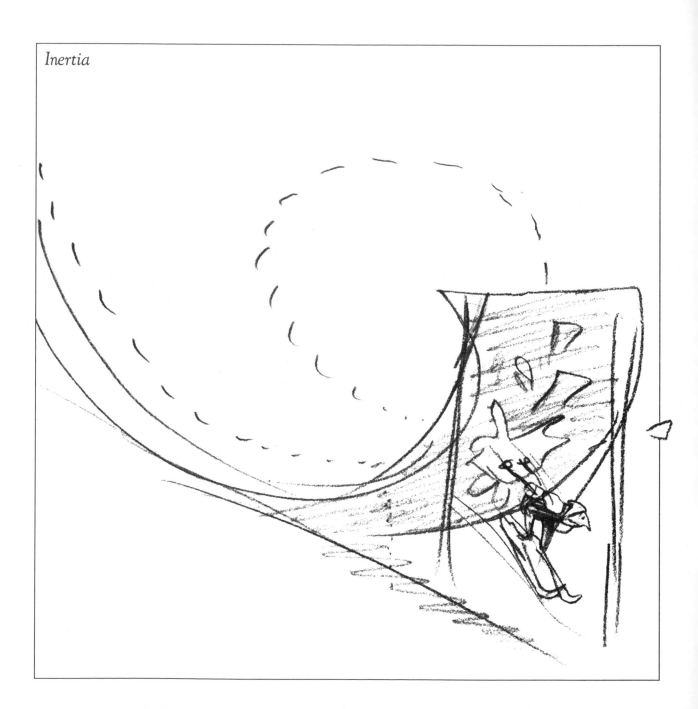

Inertia

Hotdogging   Term for freestyle acrobatic skiing, done on a slope or from a jump on special skis, with demanding aerial movements like the Outrigger, the Backscratcher, the Moebius Flip, the Space Walk, and the Wongbanger. *See* HOTFOOTING.

Hotfooting   Term for freestyle ski-boot walking, done on snow, icy pavement, or stairs while carrying a pair of skis over the shoulder, with demanding terrestrial movements like the Moon Walk, the Gulag Shuffle, the Frankenstein Stomp, the Step Slip, the Pole Trip, and the Shinbanger.

Hoting Ski   The earliest known ski, a short, wide, quite crude and inefficient-looking slab of slightly curved and pointed pine wood with slits for some sort of strap. About 4,500 years old, it was unearthed from a peat bog in Sweden. Only one ski of the pair was found, along with a twisted piece of mangled iron, the equally primitive Hoting Ski Lock.

Hot Tub   Circular therapeutic bathing pool where, after a long day on the slopes, skiers can get into hot water with their loved ones or get into hot water with their loved ones.

I

Ice   *See* FEAR.

Inertia   The tendency of a skier's body to resist changes in direction or speed due to the action of Newton's First Law of Motion. Other physical laws that affect skiers include:
- Two objects of greatly different mass falling side by side will have the same rate of descent, but the lighter one is going to have larger hospital bills.
- Matter can be neither created nor destroyed, but if it

drops out of a parka pocket, don't expect to encounter it again in our universe.

- No two bodies can occupy precisely the same location at exactly the same time unless the gondola loader is a true professional.
- Every action taught by one ski instructor is opposed by an equally qualified ski instructor with an opposite point of view.
- When an irresistible force meets an immovable object, an unethical lawyer will immediately appear.
- Even though there is no such thing as perpetual motion, it is definitely not a good idea to stand still after getting off the chairlift.
- What goes up, must wait.
- A body at rest will continue at rest even after it is acted upon by an outside force unless that force opens the blinds, turns the radio on loud and takes away the covers.

Injury   Physical harm or damage suffered as the result of a skiing accident. Past studies seem to show that injuries are most common on that "one last run of the day" when skiers are tired and their concentration is poor. New evidence suggests, however, that it is when they are incompletely warmed up, overeager, and impulsive that skiers run the greatest risk of suffering a mishap, and that consequently, if they simply eliminate entirely that alluring but potentially disastrous first run of the day, the chance of injury is effectively reduced to zero.

Inner Boot   The soft, pliable interior part of an alpine ski boot, which, if it didn't pinch, would keep the foot, if the right socks had been worn, firmly and comfortably in place if the outer shell didn't bind. *See* OUTER SHELL, SOCK.

Inside Ski

Inside Ski Term used by instructors for the ski on the inside of any turn which is also the downhill ski at the start of the turn, the uphill ski at the end of the turn, and the outside ski in the next turn. Students refer to it by a more informal term like "the ski that thingees on the whatsis." *See* OUTSIDE SKI.

J

J-bar A drag lift that can trip, snag, sideswipe, wrench, flip, bonk, bash, or clobber only one skier at a time. *See* T-BAR.

Jet Turn *1.* A turn that is initiated by propelling the feet forward. *2.* A turn that is canceled because of equipment problems, or is made with an intermediate unplanned stop, or is diverted to an unintended destination.

K

Kick Turn A technique for making a 180° turn while standing on a slope in which the skier lifts and pivots the skis, one by one, until they are both pointed in the opposite direction from their original position. It's a complicated and awkward maneuver, and so most skiers save up all their really sharp stationary turns for a rest stop in the middle or at the end of the day when they can take off their skis and just twirl around a few times on their way to the bathroom.

Kinderski Common, generic term for a special children's ski school in a resort area. Even very small children learn to ski quickly and easily, but fortunately for the adults whom they leave behind on the slopes in a cloud of powder, they have much more difficulty mastering other equally important aspects of the skiing experience: for example, they have a great deal of trouble climbing barstools; few of them can fill out a credit card voucher, even with a crayon; none of them knows the difference between pasta and pesto; and most of them would drown in a hot tub.

Klister	A thick ski wax that comes out of the tube in a klumsy klotted klump of klinging krud.
Knapsack	A bag used by skiers to carry around a large knumber of things knobody ever ends up kneeding.

L

Layering	Putting on several relatively thin overlapping items of clothing, one over the other, rather than one or two thick, bulky articles. This method not only produces greater warmth, more effective protection against dampness, and superior insulation from the wind, but also increases the odds that in the faddy, fast-changing world of ski styles, something that you're wearing on some part of your body will be in fashion for some portion of your ski trip.
Lift Line	1. A group of people waiting their turn to board a ski lift. 2. An opening remark or observation used in an attempt to start a conversation with an attractive individual in a lift line, such as "You know, I could spot it a mile away—you're an outdoorsy sort of person, aren't you?" or "Isn't that a coincidence—we both seem to be wearing the same number of skis!" or "Excuse me, I'm new to this—what is all this white powdery stuff around here?"

Loipeslop

Lift Pass   A pass that provides unlimited use of a ski area's lift facilities for a fixed period of time ranging from a week to a whole skiing season. A few resorts with steep, ungroomed slopes and a poor history of lift safety also offer lifetime passes, usually at about one-half the cost of a season pass.

Lift Ticket   A small card, often adhesive, that permits a skier to ride the lifts for several days, or a single day, or a half-day. Because of complaints about overcrowding, many ski areas now suspend sales of day tickets when the number of skiers on the slopes reaches some set figure, usually the height of the mountain in inches or the weight of available slope-grooming machinery in ounces, whichever is larger.

Lodge   *1.* The main building at a ski area, or a hotel in a ski resort village. *2.* The size of boot worn by a skier from New York or New Jersey with big feet.

Loipe   A set of parallel cross-country skiing tracks made in the snow by a special trail-preparation machine.

Loipeslop   A cross-country skiing track after being driven over by a snowmobile.

Long Johns   Familiar term for full-body underwear. Also known as Short Johns, Weird Johns, Incredible Shrinking Johns, and The Things That Came from the Laundromat.

M

Maze   Path indirect by a line followed that and often confusing to a chairlift leads the.

The Lodge

A View of the Slopes

Conviviality in the Lounge

EASY ACCESS TO THE LIFTS

CAMARADERIE

SERVICE

Metric Measures

Because of Europe's early domination of the sport, most skiing measurements are made in the metric system, and skiers not familiar with it should learn a few of the most useful conversions and terms:

RESORT ACCOMMODATIONS
$200 per night = 20 dekasmackers
$1,000 per night = 1 kilospondulic

PARKING AREAS
1 Buick = 2 Toyotas
1 centimeter scratch = 1 kilodamn

GRATUITIES TO RUDE SKI VILLAGE EMPLOYEES
Small tip = 1 microsimoleon
Very small tip = 1 nanodinero
Extremely small tip = 1 picomazuma

SKI GARMENT SIZE CONVERSIONS
(U.S.) Too Large = (Eur.) Perfeck feet—eet must give you ze room to move, yes no?
(U.S.) Too small = (Eur.) Perfeck feet—eet should be, how you say, snug, yes no?

LIFT-LINE WAITS
15 minutes = 1 hectovex
30 minutes = 1 megabore
45 minutes = 1 gigadrag

SLOPE GRADIENTS
1 qualm = 10 fidgets
1 funk = 100 jitters
1 phobia = 1,000 willies

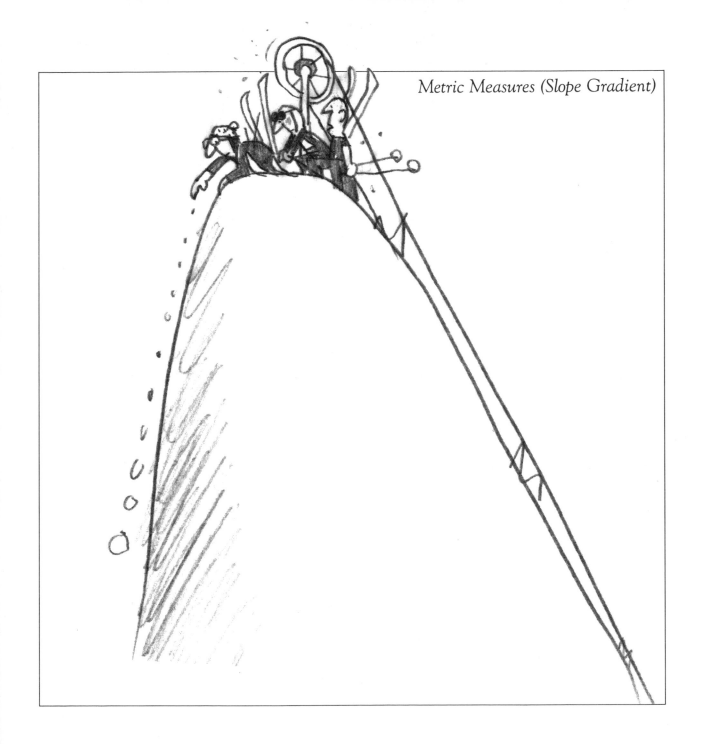

Microclimates

TEMPERATURE IN CENTIGRADE
-15° to -5° = freezing cold
-5° to 0° = freezing cold
0° = freezing cold

BROCHURE DISTANCES
Immediately adjoining = 250 meters
Right around the corner = 750 meters
Just a short ride away = 5 kilometers

LIQUID MEASURE
1 sixpack = 1 hexbox

EQUIPMENT WEIGHT
1 glove = 5 milliboots

INTERNATIONAL SKI BEHAVIOR BASED ON THE ITALIAN STANDARD
1 Scandinavian = .00004 Italians
1 Swiss = .0008 Italians
1 Austrian = .05 Italians
1 German = .3 Italians
1 Frenchman = .6 Italians
1 American college student at spring break =
    14.5 Italians

Microclimates	Weather conditions can vary dramatically over surprisingly small areas in a mountain environment, and skiers should always be prepared to adjust to these changes. For example, on a day in February when it is 25° and windy at the top of the mountain, it may be late fall around your waist, a tropical afternoon in the Amazon basin in your gloves, an early spring day with heavy showers under your turtleneck, and midnight on the dark side of Pluto at your toes.

Mitten	A large shoe worn on the hand.
Mogul	A bump or mound of snow formed by the turning action of skis in soft snow. The word was once thought to be derived from *mugel*, a regional alpine word for a hump or knoll, but it seems more likely that it actually came from *meugul*, an unexpected or unpleasant surprise; *mogolungen*, to turn upside down; *gehmogell*, to curse or use bad language; or *moogal*, a large bruise.
Mountain	The word used to describe a bump or mound of snow at ski areas in the midwestern U.S. and the Canadian plains.

N

Night Skiing	A form of skiing done after dark on specially illuminated slopes that makes it possible for skiers to be skiing at the same time that they're having a skiing nightmare.
Nordic Ski	Long, narrow, lightweight ski designed to alternately grip and glide over the snow surface when its base is coated with waxes other than the ones you happen to have on hand.
Nordic Ski Bindings	Metal clamping device of various designs and widths affixed to cross-country skis which will hold firmly in place the toe tabs of a pair of boots other than the ones you are wearing.
Nordic Ski Boot	Lightweight lace-up boot designed to attach to a nordic ski binding at the front but be free at the rear to provide enough movement to permit a blister to form on the heel while still producing sufficient constriction to allow a bruise to develop just over the middle joint of the big toe.

Mogul

Nursery Slope

Norheim, Sondre Mid-19th-century Norwegian skiing visionary who made a number of key contributions to the sport: the shorter, "waisted" ski, which made it possible to execute tighter, sharper turns; the fixed-heel binding, which made it possible for relative novices to master skiing; the parallel christie turn, which made it possible to stop quickly; and the basic slalom movement and competitive ski jumping, both of which ultimately made it possible for millions of people to stay in warm houses and watch other people ski on TV.

Nursery Slope A gentle slope reserved for beginning skiers. It is so named because in such areas there is a great deal of whining and crying, most of the motion is done on all fours, everyone needs a nap, everyone wants to go home, and no one can figure out how to go to the bathroom.

Outer Shell The hard, plastic exterior part of an alpine ski boot which, if it weren't a size too large, would hold the lower leg, if the ski pants were worn correctly, tightly in place without chafing the shins, if the inner boot hadn't worn thin and couldn't be replaced because it was discontinued by the manufacturer. *See* INNER BOOT, SOCK.

Outside Ski Term used by instructors for the ski on the outside of any turn which starts off by being the uphill ski but ends up becoming both the downhill ski and the inside ski of a new turn. It is referred to by students as "the oh who the hell cares what you call the stupid thing it doesn't do what I want it to and all it does is try to trip me ski."

P

Package Tour	A plan offered by many ski resorts in which the price for lodging also includes, at no extra charge, transportation to and from the rooms by high-speed elevator or reliable, easy-to-use stairs; all-day room key storage "on the house"; free use of après-ski hot tubs, hot showers, and hot sinks; and complimentary lessons in the lobby on basic ski techniques, like standing in line and paying for things.
Pain	*See* BOOT.
Parallel Turn	The most difficult, stylish, and professional-looking motion in skiing, in which the skis are tightly aligned and exactly equidistant throughout an entire turn. Keeping the skis perfectly parallel during turns is the goal of most amateurs, and it is one they have no difficulty achieving on the long, winding runs to and from resort areas when their skis are neatly and precisely lined up in racks attached to the roofs of their cars.
Parka	The larval stage of a blimp.
Piste	*1. (n.)* A hard-packed trail. *2. (adj.)* Very angry, as when one is hit from behind when skiing on a hard-packed trail.
Pole Plant	*1.* The motion a skier makes in placing the ski pole into the snow to facilitate a turn. *2.* A climbing flower or vegetable trained to grow up a ski pole by a former skier who has elected to pursue a more rewarding pastime.
Poles	Pointed metal sticks carried by skiers to ensure that they will have something hard and sharp to land on even if they fall on a perfectly groomed bunny slope.

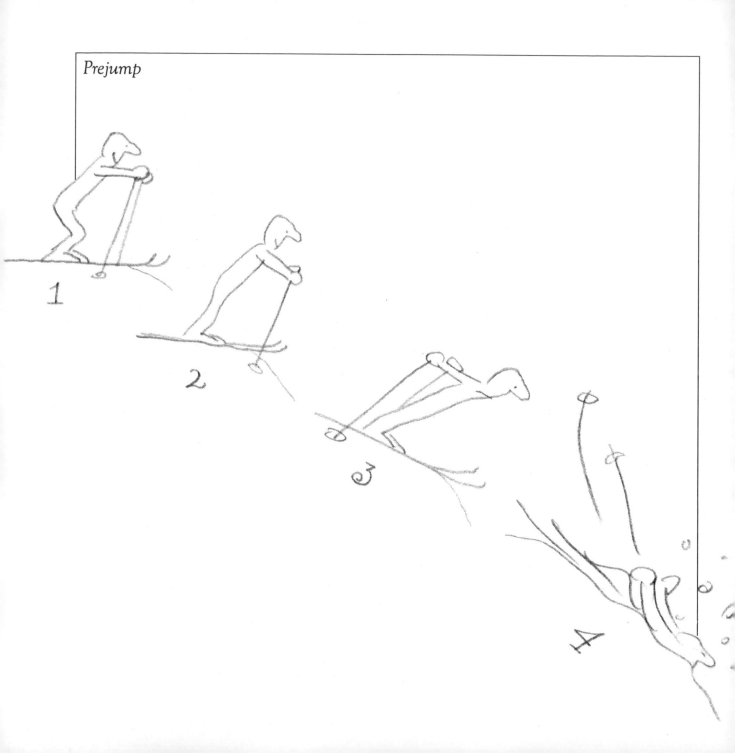

Prejump

1

2

3

4

Pole Strap
A leather or fabric loop attached to the grip on a ski pole. Whether you loop the straps around your wrists or not depends largely on whether, following a fall, you wish to risk losing your poles or prefer to risk knowing precisely where your poles are without even seeing them.

Polyethylene
A synthetic substance used for ski bases which, along with the polyurethane employed in ski boots and the polypropylene found in ski garments, has revolutionized skiing in the last decade. Among the new artificial materials that promise similar advances in the sport in the years to come are polyindigestylene, a styrene sandwich filling now being tested at ski slope lunchspots; polynothine, a polymer resin that will shortly replace the few remaining natural fibers in ski hotel bed and bath linens, fulfilling the age-old hotelier's dream of a towel no thicker than a human hair; and polyexorbitane, a thermoplastic that will make it possible for every single item sold in resort village ski shops to be molded from the same lightweight, breakable substance.

Pomalift
A ski lift that consists of a series of steel rods with disks on the end that skiers straddle one by one, tuck between their legs, and ride uphill. "Poma" comes from Jean Pomagalski, who stumbled on its design by accident in 1946 while trying to devise an automatic spanking machine for the French school system.

Prejump
A maneuver in which an expert skier makes a controlled jump just ahead of the point where he or she would be thrown upwards by a bump or slope crest. Beginners in a similar situation can execute a controlled prefall just before losing their balance and precede it with a prescream, a precurse, and a few pregroans or premoans.

Q

Quad Chairlift	A high-speed ski lift that has the capacity to carry in a single chair unit all the individuals needed for a complete, self-contained skiing mishap at the unloading point, including the skier who makes the impact, the skier who trips him, the skier he hits, and one witness.

R

Racing Ski	A ski used by experts in competitions such as downhill racing, the slalom, and the giant slalom. *See* RECREATIONAL SKI.
Recreational Ski	A ski used by intermediate skiers on an everyday basis or for a particular type of sport skiing, such as bump skiing or powder skiing. *See* RENTAL SKI.
Rental Ski	A ski used by beginners for downhill falling, the slam, and the giant slam after it has been used by a more advanced skier for stump skiing, root skiing, and rock skiing.
Retaining Strap	A strap connecting the skier's leg to the binding so that the ski remains attached to the skier during a fall; sometimes referred to as a "safety strap," but more commonly known as a "death thong," a "snuff leash," a "croak cord," a "zap strap," a "waste lace," or "doom twine."
Rill	*1.* (Nordic skiing) *n.* A very fine lengthwise groove cut into the base of a ski. *2.* (California skiing) *adv.* Very or truly, as in "the snow was rill fine."

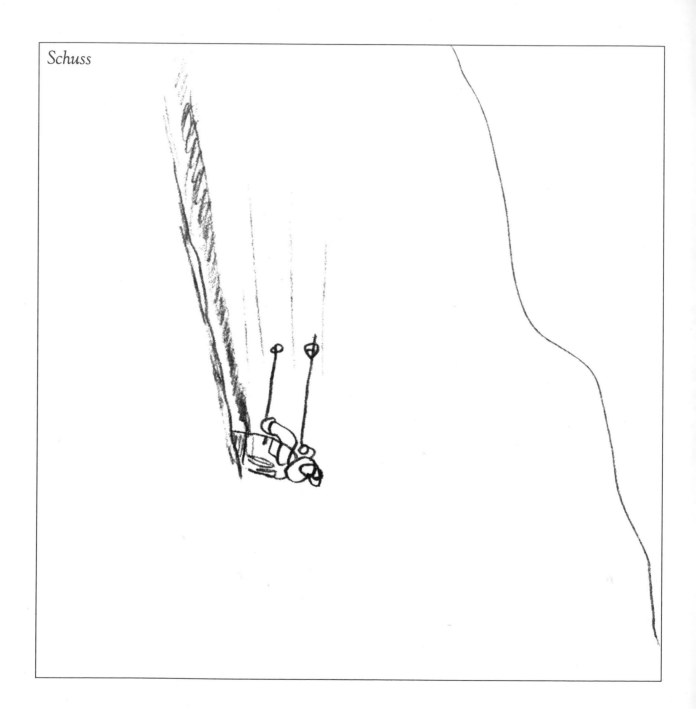

Schuss

Rope Tow	The simplest ski lift, consisting of a continuously moving rope that skiers grab onto in order to be pulled uphill. Rope tows cause sore arms and shredded gloves, but when they are running properly they don't produce horrible lift lines, and if they break suddenly they don't produce horrible headlines.

S

Schuss	An onomatopoetic German word for a fast, straight run directly down the fall line. If the skier makes it all the way to the bottom of the hill, it is a *schwhew*; if he runs into a snowbank, it is a *schmuff*; if he falls down, it is a *schwhump*; if he hits an obstacle, it is a *schmack*; if he collides with another skier, it is a *schlamm-bamm*; and if he goes off the marked run completely and into the woods, it is a *schwhoosh-schmush-schplatt*.
Schussboomer	A thoughtless and reckless skier; a schitthead.
Shin	The bruised area on the front of the leg that runs from the point where the ache from the wrenched knee ends to the place where the soreness from the strained ankle begins.
Short-ski Teaching Method	A ski instruction system that makes it possible for a beginner to progress in just a few days from 100cm skis to 150cm crutches.
Shovel	*1.* The upwardly curved and pointed front part of a ski. *2.* A necessary tool when all that is visible protuding from the snow following a skier's fall in deep powder or after an avalanche is the flat, squared-off, slightly upturned rear part, or "tail," of the skis.

Side-slipping

A method of descending a steep slope in a controlled sideways skid initiated by flattening the skis and usually completed by flattening other skiers.

Side-stepping

A method of ascending a steep slope by setting the skis into the snow in a series of short parallel steps initiated with a motion exactly like climbing a flight of stairs sideways and usually completed with a motion exactly like falling down a flight of stairs sideways.

Sitzmark

A German word for the imprint in the snow made by a fallen skier.

Sitzremark

An Anglo-Saxon word uttered by a falling skier.

Skating

A technique in which a skier moves forward over flat ground by stepping from one ski to another, pushing off strongly from the edges. Its chief value is for the absent-minded or altitude-dazed amateur winter sports enthusiast who arrives at an ice rink with a pair of skis or who discovers in the lift line that he is the only person with a hockey stick.

Ski Brake

A spring-loaded device attached to the ski that digs a pair of prongs into the snow to hold the ski in place after it is released during a fall. Ski brakes and other improvements like Teflon anti-friction pads and standardized binding settings have done much to reduce the number of ski injuries, but the search for even greater safety continues, and the future may bring a self-inflating parka air bag, battery-powered turn signals for ski poles, a powerful air-horn that can be worn on the wrist, and a 2% tax on day-glo ski clothing to create a fund to provide snowboarders with all-expense-paid ski trips to the Lebanese alps.

Ski² Length

Ski Bum
Someone who, because he would rather ski than work, takes a low-paying job at a ski resort so that he can watch people with high-paying jobs ski while he is working.

Ski Bunny
An attractive young woman who hangs around ski resorts; a snow bimbo; a slope tart; a mogul slut; a schuss hussy; a slalom trollop; a ramp tramp; a lift chippy; a lodge doxy; a jacuzzi floozy.

Ski Construction
Skis have undergone considerable technological refinement in the past two decades, and the would-be purchaser can easily become confused by terms like "torsion box," "foam core," "A.B.S. top surface," "epoxy fiberglass layer," "firm forebody," "slalom action," and "medium heel," but all a skier really has to be able to recognize is the two different types of ski salesmen: Ultra-Slime (polyester outer covering, slippery exterior, synthetic smile, maximum pressure, high-volume action, artificial hairpiece, rotten core, total heel) and Rocky Mountain Air-Head (natural fiber covering, strong background, no rough edges, easy manner, moderate flexibility, limited fact grasp, short attention span, slow uptake, slack jaw).

Skier
One who pays an arm and a leg for the opportunity to break them.

Ski Length
A simple computation based on a standard scale that takes into account your height, weight, and experience makes it easy to select the ski length that is right for you. However, when considering whether to rent or purchase skis, it is worth remembering that your ideal ski length will change if, as a result of skiing regularly, you gain experience, or lose weight, or, in extreme instances, lose height.

Ski Lift

An uphill transportation system in a ski area; sometimes a surface or drag lift, but in North America usually an open chairlift or enclosed cable car. There is a pair of basic distinctions between the way these two types of aerial lifts operate. The first is that in the chairlift you develop a cold directly from exposure to freezing winds while seated in an unprotected chair, whereas in the cable car one is given to you by the people coughing and sneezing in a stuffy gondola cabin. The second distinction is that as you leave the chairlift, it is up to you to injure yourself by falling down on the unloading ramp, but as you exit the cable car, someone will do this for you, either by kicking you in the shins with a ski boot, sticking you in the side with a ski pole, or bashing you on the back of the head with a pair of skis.

Ski Pants

1. Trousers designed to be worn while skiing, often made of a skintight stretch material. *2.* Nonverbal expressions of lust for an attractive fellow skier of the opposite sex wearing skintight ski pants.

Ski Patrol

A group of trained, experienced volunteers or professionals, wearing distinctive parkas with white crosses, who are responsible for the maintenance of safety, the elimination of dangerous conditions, and the treatment of injuries in ski areas. A note to skiers: Although members of the ski patrol are prepared to respond instantly in any emergency, a broken hot tub is not considered a life-threatening situation; moreover, while patrol members do have sweeping powers on the slopes, including the authority to withdraw lift privileges from reckless skiers and the sole discretion to close trails, they cannot grant divorces, order annoying children sent to reform schools, or revoke the visas of obnoxious Europeans.

Ski Lift

Slope-grooming Machine

Skis	A pair of long, thin, flexible runners that permit a skier to slide across the snow and into debt.
Ski School	A place where novices are turned into menaces.
Slalom	A competitive event in alpine skiing in which racers run a course marked out with gates that must be passed through during the descent. The word *slalom* means "slope tracks," and it comes from Norway, like many other commonly used skiing terms, including *ôöps* (a fall), *blåmmo* (a collision with a tree), *fløö* (a bad cold), *gløpp* (food served at a mountain lunchspot), *brått* (an annoying child who can ski expertly), *bjerk* (a showoff), *lyftbøöb* (someone who cuts into a lift line), and *fökkendölt* (a skier who runs into other skiers).
Sliding	A term used to describe the movement of the skis straight ahead, whether flat or on edge.
Slipping	A term used to describe movement of the skis in a sideways direction.
Slivving, Slobbling, Slonging, Slooning, Slozzling, Sluffling, Slurzing, & Sluschulling	Terms used to describe some of the many other movements skis are capable of.
Slope-grooming Machine	A large, tracked vehicle that is used to transform a slope that is unskiable because it is too deeply moguled into one that is unskiable because it is hopelessly crowded.
Snow	Form of precipitation that occurs the morning of the departure from a ski resort or three weeks prior to arrival.

Snowboard

A short, wide, ski-shaped board designed for "snow-surfing," with a flat surface on one side and a fathead on the other.

Snowplow

A ski position in which the tails are pushed out into a V-shape and the insides are edged. The snowplow is the first maneuver on skis taught to beginners once they've mastered basic movements like the Snowsit, the Snowfall, the Snowchew, and the Abominable Snowman.

Snowplow Turn

A slow, safe, easily controlled turning method based on edging and wedging the skis that is used to teach beginners how to change direction so they get enough confidence to ski down the fall line and thus achieve the first level of skill in skiing: the ability to trip and fall over objects other than those they brought with them. *See* STEM TURN.

Snow Snake

An invisible but malevolent creature whom skiers blame for causing their falls. Other troublesome unseen slope dwellers include the rack rat, who knocks over carefully propped-up skis; the pole cat, who snatches ski poles from skiers' hands just as the chairlift starts and flings them into the snow below; the piste weasel, who momentarily obscures or reverses trail-marking signs; and the powder parrot, whose weird squawks make it appear that an exasperated skier has just said something extremely crude.

Sock

Woven foot covering made of silk, wool, or artificial fibers. The formula for determining how many pairs of which type of sock to wear is simple: The ideal fit in a ski boot is always achieved with a combination of socks that have two-thirds the thickness of any two pairs or one-third more thickness than any one pair.

Stem Turn

I   II   III   IV   V

Stance

The correct stance is an essential part of skiing. Your knees should be flexed, but weak and shaking slightly; your ankles should be bent and wobbly; your feet should be slightly apart and quaking noticeably in your boots; your arms should be straight and covered with a good layer of gooseflesh; your hands should be forward, your palms clammy, your knuckles white, and your fingers icy; your upper body should be upright and bathed in sweat, your stomach sinking; your hips should be forward and swaying nervously from side to side; your head should be up, your eyes a little crossed and darting in all directions; your mouth should be open, your lips quivering, and you should be mumbling audibly "No, no, *no*" or "Why, *why?*"

STAR Test

The Standard Rating Test, a uniform scoring system that helps skiers determine their skill level. There are six levels of proficiency: expert (gold), intermediate (silver), novice (bronze), dunce (iron), nitwit (tin), and boob (lead).

Star Turn

1. A stationary turn on flat ground in which the skier pivots the ski tips around the tails, or the tails around the tips, in a circular motion. *2.* A stationary turn in which a skier sharply pivots the head and upper body to see if that really is Robert Redford skiing by.

Stem Turn

A somewhat more difficult turn than the snowplow that involves pushing out the tail of one ski into a half-snowplow, then bringing the other ski alongside of it. It is taught to intermediate skiers so that they can gain enough confidence to ski across and down a slope with their skis parallel and thus achieve the second level of skill in skiing: the ability to crash into another skier rather than waiting for another skier to crash into them. *See* STEP TURN.

Step Turn

A still more difficult technique for changing direction in which the weight is taken completely off one ski and transferred onto the other during the turn. It is taught to advanced skiers so that they can make uphill traverses and ski faster and thus achieve the third level of skiing skill: the ability to crash into skiers slightly higher on the slope than they are, as well as skiers below them, and the ability to crash into more than one skier at any one time.

Summer Skiing

It is possible to ski in the northern hemisphere during the warmer months, either on "dry" slopes covered with artificial skiing surfaces or on "grass" skis with wheels that permit ski-like motions on unaltered hillsides. However, since neither of these is a satisfactory substitute for the real thing, many skiers have taken up golf, often playing at one of the excellent courses in ski resort areas. Although "the slopes" and "the links" may not appear to have much in common, they share a surprising number of features, a fact that no doubt explains the powerful attraction of golf to skiers:

• Expensive, cumbersome equipment
• Tasteless, silly clothing
• Astronomical fees for daily outings
• Long waits due to crowds
• An awkward bent-knee stance and strange, illogical body-twisting movements
• Baffling and contradictory instruction
• Mean-spirited competition
• A reasonable risk of serious injury
• Frequent searches for lost things
• Unpredictable weather
• Tiresome know-it-alls eager to impart advice

T

T-bar	A drag lift that can accommodate two skiers. A word of warning to individuals unfamiliar with the T-bar system: it starts with a jerk, and, if you're skiing alone, you are likely to end up riding it with a jerk.
Teaching System	A formal method of ski instruction designed to ensure that students always know the correct terms for their mistakes, the proper names for the rules they're breaking, and the right reasons why everything they're doing is wrong.
Telemark Turn	A demanding nordic skiing technique in which the skier advances the outside ski, drops into a kneeling position, and then stems and edges this leading, steering ski into a wide, graceful turn that ends with a smooth recovery into a new traverse. *See* TELEPARK TURN.
Telepark Turn	A demanding ski-area driving technique in which the motorist makes a sudden, sharp turn to steer his vehicle into a position that will permit another car to leave a parking place while blocking anyone else from edging forward and taking it before he can slip smoothly into it.
Terrain	A given ski area, considered in terms of its steepness, the irregularity of its surface, the sharpness of its contours, the presence of obstacles, and the severity of the risk in skiing it. *See* TERROR.
Terror	Appropriate reaction after considering the terrain.
Theory	In skiing, an incomprehensible explanation for a series of unwarranted conclusions based on inaccurate observations of irrelevant details.

Thor	Thcandinavian god of acheth and painth. *Thee* ULLR.
Tilting	Leaning or banking into a slope during a turn or traverse. If this motion is overdone, unfortunate results may occur.
Tip	*1.* The front end, or "shovel," of the ski, which curves sharply upward and comes to a point. *2.* A piece of advice or information, such as "Excuse me, but inasmuch as the front ends of your skis neither curve sharply upward nor come to a point, I conclude that you have them on backwards." *3.* A small gratuity conferred for a kindness, as in "Here is a round metal coin with a milled edge and a raised-relief design on both sides which I offer to you in return for your assistance."
Toboggan	A wide, flat-bottomed sled used by the ski patrol to transport injured skiers down the slopes. Its name comes from a Micmac Indian phrase, *Toh-pah-kinn,* whose closest English equivalent is "So long, sucker."
"Track Left" & "Track Right"	Shouts made by someone descending a slope to let people on the trail ahead know that a skier is coming down the hill. Two other warnings that skiers should be familiar with are "Ski!", which alerts those on the slope below that a loose ski is coming down the hill, and "Avalanche!", which tells everyone that a hill is coming down the hill.
Trail	A place where the lift line moves a little faster.
Trail Map	An accurately scaled, color-coded representation of the layout and location of all the trails, lifts, and other facilities of the area you are skiing, printed on a sheet of durable, foldable glossy paper that is in the pocket of an article of clothing you decided not to wear today.

Tip

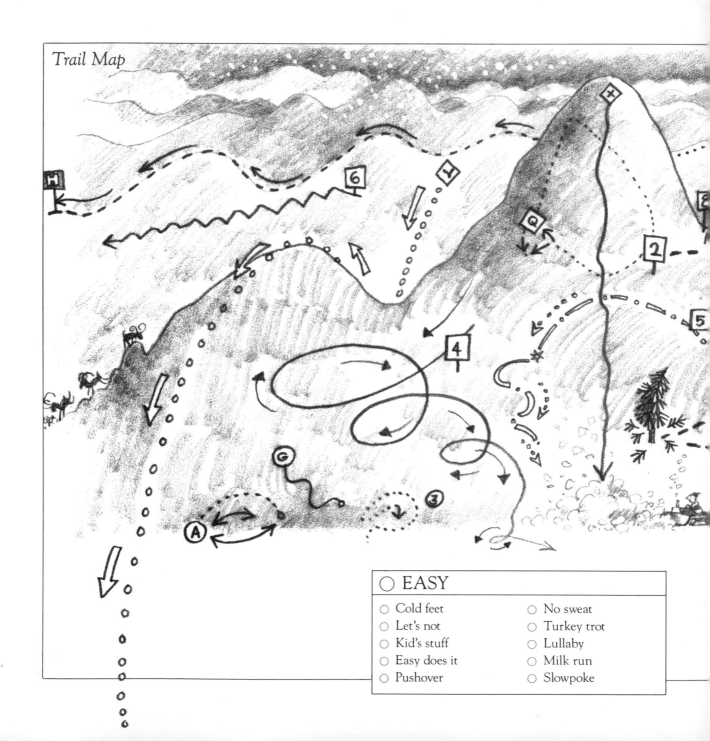

Trail Map

○ EASY

○ Cold feet	○ No sweat
○ Let's not	○ Turkey trot
○ Kid's stuff	○ Lullaby
○ Easy does it	○ Milk run
○ Pushover	○ Slowpoke

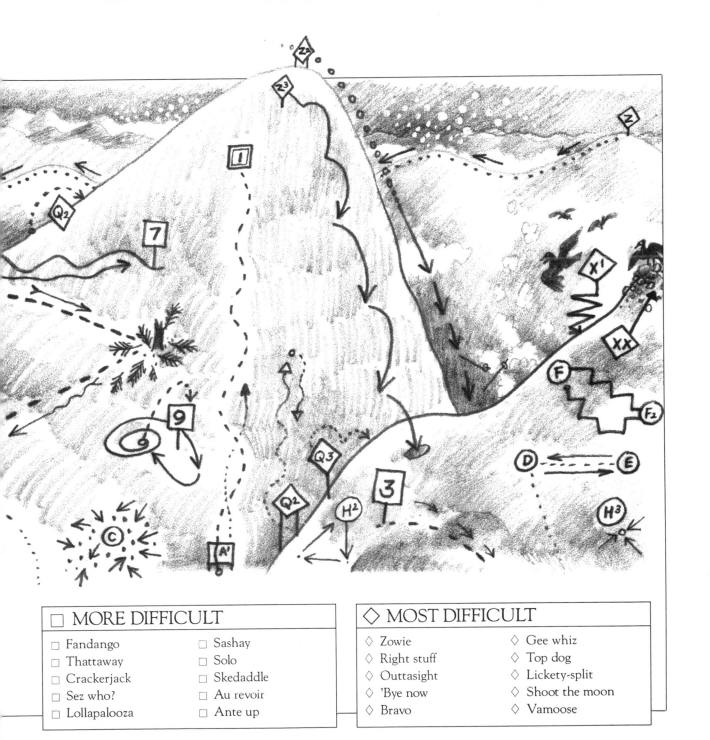

Tuning Skis

Trail Rating	Ski slopes in North America are marked with a green circle for the easiest, a blue square for the more difficult, and one or two black diamonds for the most difficult. However, since slope grading is not an exact science, many "green" slopes have "blue" areas, and a lot of "blue" slopes have "black" areas, and consequently most skiers also have black and blue areas.
Traversing	Skiing across a slope at an angle to the fall line: one of two quick and simple methods of reducing speed and/or coming to a complete stop on a trail or run.
Tree	The other method.
Tuning Skis	Flattening, smoothing, and waxing the bases and sharpening the edges of a pair of skis to eliminate concavity (which makes them "hooky" or "grabby") or convexity (which makes them "squirrely"). Skiers can do this themselves (which makes them "cranky," "grouchy," or "crabby"), or they can pay a fairly stiff fee to have it done at a ski shop (which makes them "sulky" or "orncry").
Turn	Any change in the position of the skis that leads to a change in direction, a change of clothes or equipment, or, in extreme cases, a change in vacation plans.
Two-piece Ski Suit	*1.* A type of ski wear with separate jacket and pants. *2.* A type of personal injury litigation with two separate complaints against one skier or complaints against two separate skiers.
Two-wax System	A simplified waxing procedure for nordic skis that uses just two waxes—one for below freezing and one for above—to produce the entire range of horrible tracking conditions that it once took over a dozen different waxes to achieve.

U

Ullr	Scandinavian deity and pagan patron saint of skiers, condominium salesmen, and orthopedic surgeons.
Unweighting	A quick upward or downward movement of the hips, knees, and ankles at the beginning of a turn, which, if done properly, takes some of the skier's weight off the skis momentarily, making turning easier, and if done improperly, takes all of the skier's weight off the skis, transferring it temporarily to the hips, knees, elbows, arms, or head.
Up	The direction in skiing in which nothing goes by itself, except prices.

V

Vertical Drop or Rise	The maximum length of skiable downhill terrain at any given resort area as measured from a skier standing at the foot of the offloading ramp at the end of the highest lift on the summit to the glove, pole, hat, or wallet he dropped into deep snow at the very beginning of the first lift at the base of the mountain.

W

Warming Hut	A convivial shelter on the slopes where skiers can get together, drink hot chocolate, and swap colds.

Warm-weather Skiing Conditions

POWDER

SLUSH

HARD PACK

Warm-weather Skiing Conditions	Tricky skiing environment encountered in late winter and early spring when, due to warming weather, the trail surfaces can be covered with crust or "crud," granular or "corn" snow, patches of ice or "boilerplate," and slush or "mashed potatoes," and, because of Easter vacation, the trails are filled with partying students or "scumballs," obnoxious children or "creeps," out-of-practice once-a-year skiers or "mogul bait," and fallen beginners or "slope potatoes."
Water Skiing	The only form of skiing in which skiers can't end up by accident in a place that is too steep for them, don't always wish they were wearing a lot more or a lot less clothing, never have to worry about ice, and won't ever run into a Swiss kindergarten student who is a hundred times better than they are.
Waxing Skis	Putting wax on the bases of alpine skis to smooth out gouges and protect the surface is a useful but optional step in the ski preparation process, but it is essential to proper performance of nordic skis to apply to specific areas on their bases a glide or grip wax color-coded for the temperature it is suited for: either green, for 20° or colder, or blue, for anything up to about 30°, or red, for anything warmer. While applying these waxes, the skier himself goes through a range of colors, first getting green around the gills from inhaling wax-solvent vapors, then cursing a blue streak as he tries to get the wax to stick in the right places, then growing purple with rage as the ski backslips on the kick and grabs on the glide, and finally becoming red in the face from the heat as he stokes a stove fire hot enough to burn a pair of nordic skis.

Waxless Skis   Nordic skis with a special patterned base that ensures that they will perform unsatisfactorily even if they aren't coated with the wrong wax.

Wedel   Austrian vord for a series of short, fast, "vagging" turns in the fall line vhich are usually made right down the middle of a crowded catvalk through the voods by some half-vitted buttvipe vearing a Valkman.

Wedge   *1.* (General skiing) *n.* Another name for the snowplow ski position. *2.* (New England skiing) *adv.* + *v.* An inquiry about a particular location, as in "Wedge you buy your skis?"

X

XC   Abbreviation for cross-country skiing. The other abbreviations widely used in skiing are MC (Master Card), DC (Diner's Club), and AE (American Express).

Y

Yodel   Traditional alpine cry that shifts suddenly from an ordinary pitch to sharp, warbled falsettos. It takes years of practice to learn how to yodel properly, but an amateur can produce a remarkably convincing imitation of the real thing if, during a fairly fast downhill run, he goes off the edge of a trail and his skis pass on either side of a medium-size tree.

Wedel

Zdarsky, Mathias

Z

Zdarsky, Mathias   A turn-of-the-century Austrian skiing pioneer with an astonishing number of "firsts" to his credit, including being the first person to use the snowplow and stem turns, producing the first study of avalanches, designing the first slalom course, starting the first ski school, developing the first teaching technique (Do it, You stink, Pay me, Go away), writing the first illustrated ski manual ("Ski My Way, You Fool"), and even constructing the first hot tub (though his name for it, "The Hell Vat," proved an obstacle to its speedy popularization). Ironically, even in death he was an innovator. He perished in the world's first ski lift accident in 1933, when his ingenious Mountain Zeppelin, a series of chain-linked, cable-driven mini-blimps, exploded. He was buried, according to his wishes, on his beloved ski slopes, on a peak at the end of a funicular railway. Thousands attended his funeral, patiently waiting for their places on the cogwheel train. It was the world's first lift line.